THE TRUE SIZE OF FOOD

THE TRUE SIZE OF FOOD

By Marijke Timmerman

ABOUT OUR ABSURD WAYS WITH FOOD

BISPUBLISHERS

BIS Publishers
Building Het Sieraad
Postjesweg 1
1057 DT Amsterdam
The Netherlands
T+31(0)20 5150230
F+31(0)20 5150239
bis@bispublishers.nl
www.bispublishers.nl

ISBN 978-90-6369-349-7

CHAPTERS

i graze
he grazes
we graze

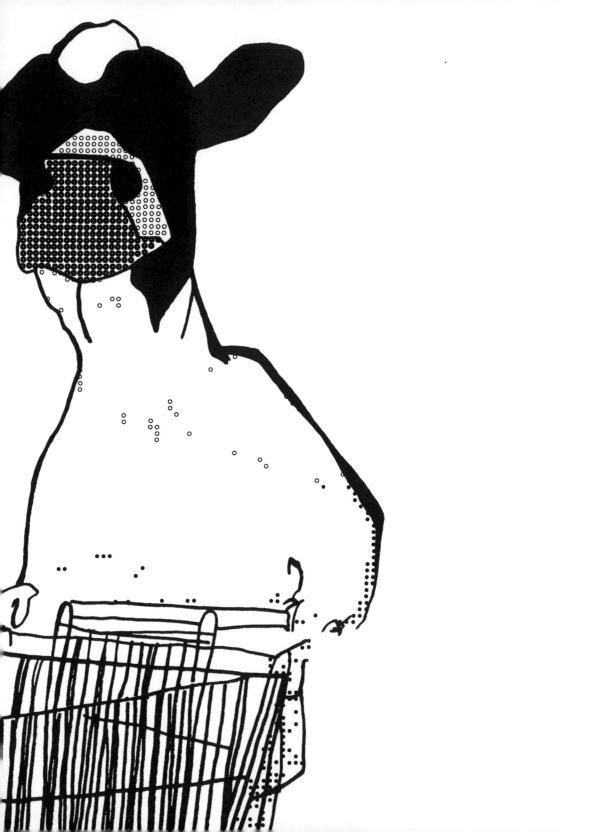

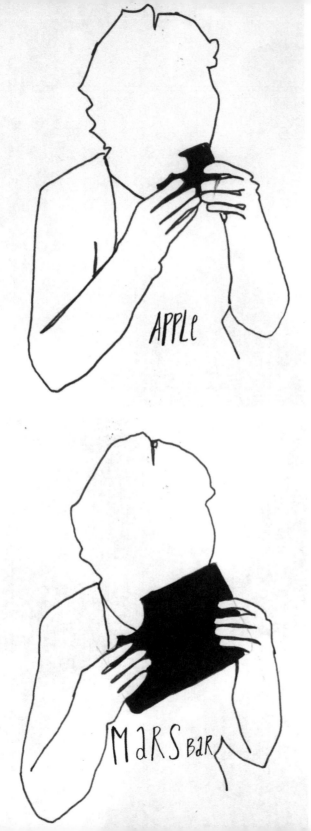

APPLe

MaRSbar

HOW DO WE Cope WITH the ABUNDANCE of FOOD?

*I*n our western society, food is sold everywhere, stores are always fully stocked, and the food is always fresh. Instead of having to hunt for our sustenance, it now actually takes effort for us to avoid it. At the same time, we are obsessed with nutrition. There currently is an explosion of diets, food gurus, low-fat products, and TV shows on weight loss. How do we respond to this excess supply of food?

The True Size of Food provides a visual representation of our absurd ways with food.

This book started out as a personal frustration of mine; why does my mind always tempt me to consume more than my body needs? Frustration over food becoming such an easily disposable product, while so many people in the world are starving. The overwhelming feeling I get when I'm standing in a supermarket, not able to choose from the vast assortment available. Wondering what influence marketeers have on our eating habits.
I started a small research project and translated my findings into visualisations. By visualising my observations and illustrating my point of view, I gained a clear insight into these questions. It increased my awareness. The reason why we eat is certainly not only in response to a physical need anymore, but also involves a psychological need. Sometimes my findings were shocking to me; at other times they were somewhat comforting. Today, I'm more aware of why, how and what I eat. I have more control over the choices I make regarding food.
I've collected all my visualisations on the subject in this book. This book is not meant to impose yet another opinion on the subject matter, nor will it tell you what to do. It will not give you pointers for a healthy lifestyle. All this book does, is provide you with a clear image and a better understanding of how we handle our food in western society.

INTRODUCTION

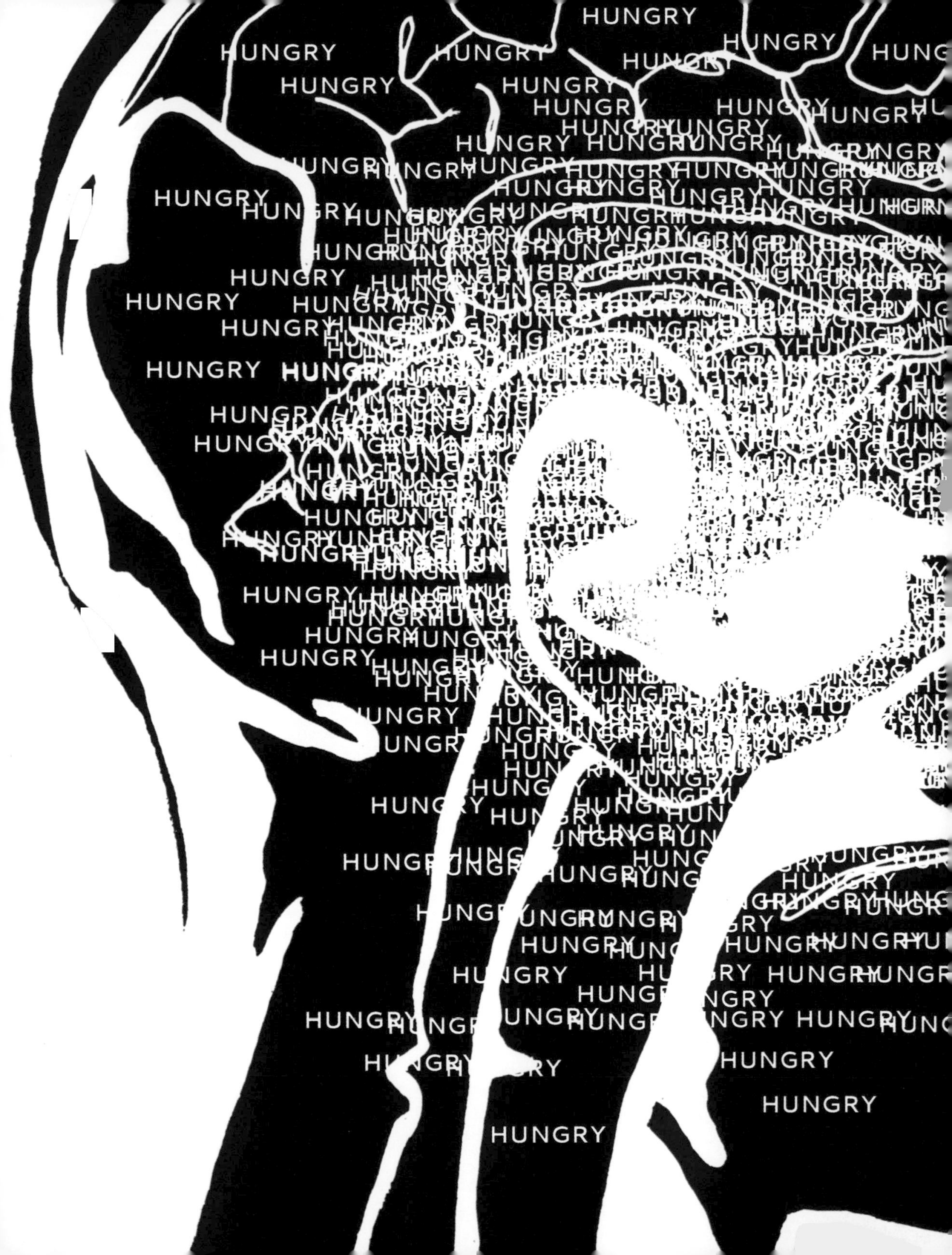
HUNGRY

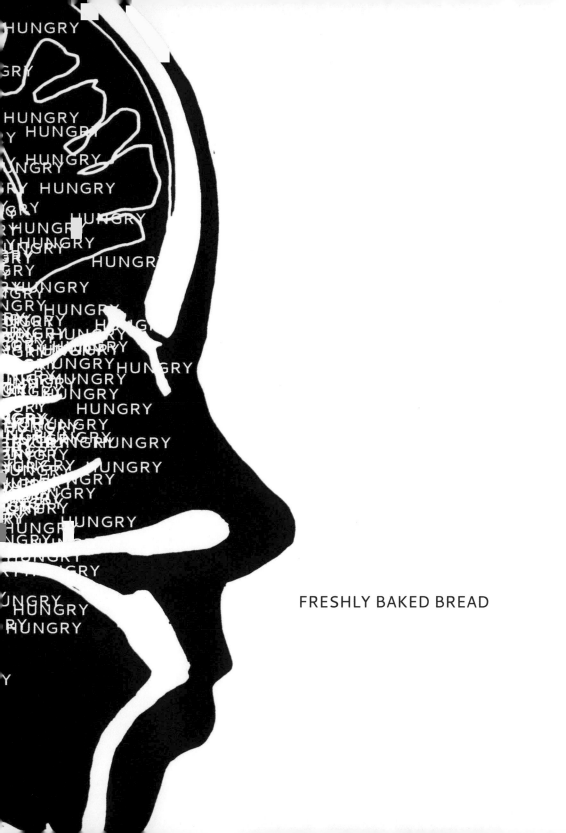

FRESHLY BAKED BREAD

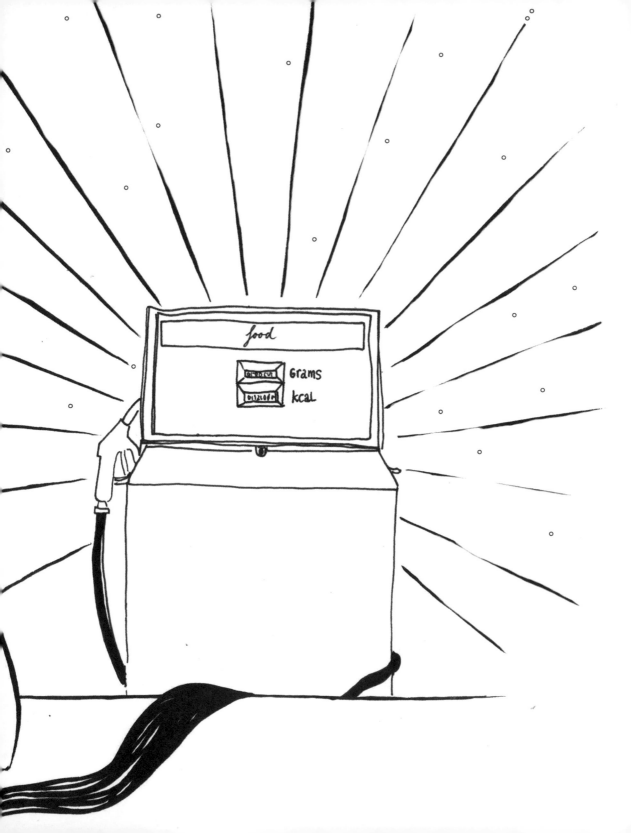

MY DOG
MUST THINK

I'm the
GREATEST
HUNTER on
EARTH ...

how Much FOOD
is AVAILABLE within
a 500-metre RADIUS?

IN A Medium-sized
EUROPEAN CITY

01 ————————

ALL AVAILABLE FOOD ESTABLISHMENTS WITHIN A 500–METRE RADIUS

Central point: Public library Eindhoven, The Netherlands

*M*an is inherently an omnivore, which makes us hunters and gatherers. For centuries, the men would go out hunting while the women gathered fruits, berries and nuts from nature.

Today, we have the food industry. Food is available ready-made and pre-shelled from the shelves in the supermarket. We no longer head into the woods to find the best berries or spend hours lying motionless in the bushes, aiming for that one small rabbit. Instead of having to hunt for our food, it actually takes us effort to avoid yummy treats!

The temptations from the food industry are everywhere. Food can be bought on every street corner, e.g. at supermarkets, kiosks, restaurants, grocers or snack bars. Woks to Walk, coffees to go and 1-Euro breakfasts; there is no escape.

This chapter demonstrates how overwhelming this abundance actually is by depicting all eateries located within a radius of 500 meters in the Dutch city of Eindhoven, taken as an example of an average medium-sized European city.

14 X SWEET VENDOR

19
BROOD2DAY
Nieuwe Emmasingel 11

26
Bakker Bart bakery
Demer 21

31
Subway
Vrijstraat 23

36
Broodje Smits
Wilhelminaplein 4

41
Brabantse Gebakwagen mobile bakery
Stationsplein

20
Bakkerij Bart bakery
Heuvel Galerie 10-11

27
Broodje Dubbeldik
Catharinaplein 7

32
Pain Du Délicieux
Lardinoisstraat 3

37
Pibo's
18 Septemberplein 22-A

42
Ola Happiness Station
Train station, central hall

21
Bagels & Beans
Jan van Lieshoutstraat 24

28
De Broodzaak bakery
Train station, central hall

33
Panos
Emmasingel 42

38
Bakkertje Bol bakery
Hooghuisstraat 31d

43
Ice cream parlour Bastani
De Stadspoort 2

22
't Baguetje
Begijnenhof 25-A

29
Restaurant-Cafeteria L'Escalier
Heuvel Galerie 151

34
Cafeteria Panini
Kleine Berg 79

39
Bagel and Juice
Kleine Berg 19

44
Houwen's Vlaai
Train station, central hall

24
La Place
Piazza 62

30
La Place
Heuvel Galerie 1

35
de Bijenkorf
Piazza 1

40
GoPasta Café
Catharinaplein 17

45
Gebak mobile bakery
Markt

25
Bread Box
Stationsweg 2

La Toscana ice cream van
18 Septemberplein

Ice cream parlour Roma
Heuvel Galerie 126

Soho Stationsplein
Stationsplein 15

Umi Kaiseki
Stationsplein 45

Mood
Keizersgracht 6

Toys XL
Piazza 64

Snack vending machine
Train station, central hall

Yakatori & the Sushi's
Grote Berg 30

Sang Fung
Hoogstraat 49

Japanese restaurant Kyoto
St Antoniusstraat 18

De Ijsbeer ice cream van
Crossing Demer - Vrijstraat

Service Cinema Zien
Keizersgracht 19

Nieuw Nan King
Markt 19a

Sushi Haru
Nieuwstraat 12

Restaurant Indonesia
Jan van Lieshoutstraat 22

Ice cream station Roma
Heuvel Galerie

Cinema Pathé
Dommelstraat 27

Japanese Restaurant Yokohama
Stationsplein 11

Soho
Jan van Lieshoutstraat 24A

Wokparadijs
Catharinaplein 37

Jamin confectionary
Demer 32

Coco Sushi & Noodles
Kleine Berg 149

Crystal Palace
Markt 9

Tony's Wok Away
Nieuwstraat 7/C

Take A Wok
Kleine Berg 40

Easy Wok & Go
Vestdijk 3

Si Señor
Dommelstraat 17

Tapas bar Que Pasa
Dommelstraat 19

Rodeo Eindhoven
Dommelstraat 23

Gauchos
Stationsplein 7

Sopranos
Stationsplein 9

Mexican Diner Tortillas
Dommelstraat 34

Mexican Restaurant Popocatepetl
Keizersgracht 18

Señora Rosa
Edenstraat 13

La Gitana
Kerkstraat 36

Brazilian Diner Carioca
Grote Berg 4

Sinema
Dommelstraat 25-A

Auberge Nassau
Wilhelminaplein 14

Restaurant Wiesen
Kleine Berg 10

Le Connaisseur
Kleine Berg 12

Spoon
Kleine Berg 18

Kreeftenbar
Kleine Berg 21

KB 23
Kleine Berg 23

Ribs Factory
Kerkstraat 14

Restaurant Dr. Ink
Kerkstraat 28

Restaurant Welp
Kleine Berg 35

Mangiare
Kleine Berg 67-A

Restaurant Noir
Kleine Berg 71

Restaurant Boon
Willemstraat 61

Restaurant Vlijtig Liesje
Ten Hagestraat 2

Juffrouw Tok
Edenstraat 5

Da Verdi
Dommelstraat 29

Javanese Diner
Kleine Berg 34-B

Italian Restaurant Sicilia
Dommelstraat 15

100

Sizzling Restaurant
Stationsplein 3a

101

Restaurant Claire
Kleine Berg 47

102

Memories
Dommelstraat 36

103

Restaurant-Bar 1910
Willemstraat 43 A

Ilio's
Dommelstraat 26

105

Sméagol
Kerkstraat 10

106

Restaurant De Volder
Nieuwstraat 40

107

Restaurant De Karseboom
Grote Berg 10

108

In den Bergsche tuin
Grote Berg 17

109

Greek specialities Papadopoulos
Kerkstraat 40

110

Hotel Benno
Wilhelminaplein 9

111

Hotel Sofitel Cocagne
Vestdijk 47

112

Carrousel
Markt 35

113

Eden Crown Hotel
Vestdijk 14

114

Vervoorn's vegetable and fruit grocer
Mathildelaan 13

115

Restaurant The Pancake
Nieuwstraat 74

116

Panecook
Heuvel Galerie 195

117

Bread and Pastry Bakery Hartogs
Kleine Berg 74-A

118

De Bergse Bakker bakery
Kleine Berg 77

23

ALL FOOD ESTABLISHMENTS WITHIN A 500-METRE RADIUS

119 De Minibar
Kleine Berg 60

125 't Begijntje
Stratumseind 25

131 Café Thomas
Stratumseind 23

136 Stadium Café D'n Afrap
Mathildelaan 12

141 Café Sands
Stratumseind 29

120 Café Wilhelmina
Wilhelminaplein 6

126 Café de Groot
Wilhelminaplein 8

132 Café Vlakbij
Hoogstraat 50

137 Café La Gare Du Sud
Stationsplein 22

142 Bermuda Eindhoven
Stationsplein 4

121 Club Djam
Grote Berg 12

127 Diner Publick
Markt 20

133 Café Bommel
Kleine Berg 32

138 Mundial
Dommelstraat 13

143 Café 't Mulderke
Wal 7

122 Café La Folie
Vrijstraat 40

128 Frits Philips concert hall
Jan van Lieshoutstraat 3

134 Café De Hoogste Tijd
Vrijstraat 38

139 The Rambler
Stationsplein 12

144 O'Sheas Irish Pub
Jan van Lieshoutstraat 9

123 Vijftien XV
Stratumseind 15

129 The Little One
Jan van Lieshoutstraat 26

135 Café Spijker
Stratumseind 17-21

140 Sports Bar Match
Stratumseind 27

145 Mid-City Bar
Jan van Lieshoutstraat 30

124 Hotel Queen
Markt 7

130 Sowieso
Dommelstraat 32

146 Butler & Co
Kerkstraat 18

152 Diner Anders
Grote Berg 21

158 Cooks
Kerkstraat 30

164 Diner Sjiek
Stationsplein 16

169 Newscafé
Nieuwstraat 20

147 Allicht Brasserie Stadshotel
Wilhelminaplein 3

153 Brasserie Saint Germain
Kleine Berg 57H

159 De Bengel
Stationsplein 28-29

165 Diner De Vrienden
Stationsplein 33

170 Grand Café USINE
Lichttoren 6

148 Grand Café Place Du Nord
Lardinoisstraat 2

154 Diner Movies
Vestdijk 9

160 Café Centraal
Markt 8

166 De Vooruitgang
Markt 11

171 The Peacock
Heuvel Galerie 208

149 De Gaper
Wilhelminaplein 5

155 Restaurant & Wine Bar Jiu.nu
Willemstraat 9

161 Diner D'n Bolle Boel
Stationsplein 2

167 Ons
Kerkstraat 16

172 Smalle Haven
Smalle haven 2

150 Grand Café Berlage
Kleine Berg 16

156 Dommel18
Dommelstraat 18

162 Trafalgar Pub
Dommelstraat 21

168 Book Café/Restaurant Schrijvers
Dommelstraat 24

173 Restaurant Vintage
Kerkstraat 3

151 De Wildeman
Markt 10

157 Café de Baron
Kleine Berg 26

163 Brasserie Van den Berg
Nieuwe Emmasingel 58

ALL FOOD ESTABLISHMENTS WITHIN A 500-METRE RADIUS

Night Shop
Grote Berg 49

Restaurant Aangenaam Culinair
Kleine Berg 83

KIOSK I
train station, central hall

De Tuinen
Demer 8

Fish 'n Food
Heuvel Galerie 13

Bij Uniek
Willemstraat 43

La Place panini
Vrijstraat 11

De Tuinen
Heuvel Galerie 157

Kaldi Coffee & Tea
Catharinaplein 35-A

Chocolaterie Boulanger
Hermanus Boexstraat 52

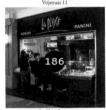

La Place Panini
Heuvel Galerie 135

Etos
Demer 2

Simon Lévelt
Heuvel Galerie 97-99

Heijmans Delicatessen
Kleine Berg 38

KIOSK II
Train station, central hall

Kruidvat
Hermanus Boexstraat 28

Wineshop Henri Bloem
Vrijstraat 10

La Semolina
Stadspoort 6

De Broodzaak bakery
Train station, central hall

Kruidvat
Rechtestraat 4

Hema
Rechtestraat 37

6 X SHAWARMA

Oriental Pizzeria & Shawarma
Nieuwstraat 9

Felfela
Lardinoisstraat 5

Grillroom Shawarma Aladin
Kleine Berg 36

Pack Döner Centrum
Dommelstraat 38-A

Grillroom - Pizzeria - Restaurant Ali Baba
Grote Berg 24

Döner Kebab
Train station, central hall

5 X COFFEE

Men's Fashion Store Ron Wildenberg
Kleine Berg 53

CaféT
Train station, central hall

Two-B by Brown's
Keizersgracht 9

Douwe Egberts shop & café
Nieuwe Emmasingel 16

Central Library Eindhoven
Emmasingel 22

3 X SUPERMARKET

Albert Heijn
18 Septemberplein 23

AH To Go
Train station, central hall

Sin Wah Supermarket
Kleine Berg 65

TOTAL: 208

27

we spend a year
60 HOURS
in a Supermar

(1)

WHAT to CHOOSE?

02 _____

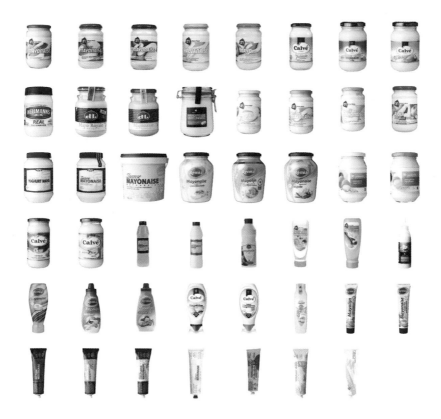

39 TYPES OF MAYONNAISE AT THE SUPERMARKET
All pictures: Albert Heijn, The Netherlands

*W*e no longer have to hunt for our food. Food is widely available and the shelves in the supermarket are always fully stocked. In fact, they offer more choices than we can handle.

The number of levorotatory or dextrorotatory yoghurts in all their shapes, sizes, flavours and fat percentages – with or without probiotics – might often leave us indecisive. How often does it take you as long as 2 minutes to choose a single product?

Analysis shows that the top four western food companies control a substantial majority of the global sales of food products, often offering multiple brands for each type of grocery which gives consumers the false impression they actually have a choice from various competing products [2]. Why are we given al these choices?

This chapter displays a collection of products, which are all available in one single grocery store.

75 TYPES OF CRISPS AT THE SUPERMARKET

44 TYPES OF MILK AT THE SUPERMARKET

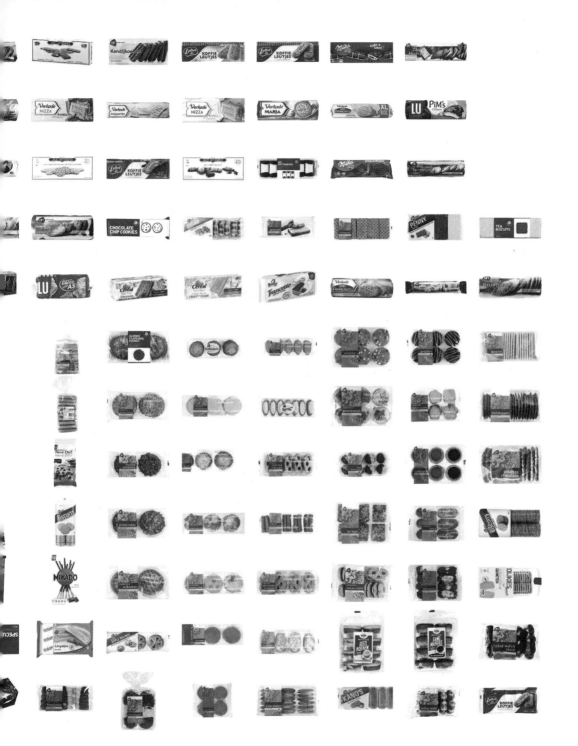

179 TYPES OF BISCUITS AT THE SUPERMARKET

59 TYPES OF MARMALADE AT THE SUPERMARKET

57 TYPES OF RICE AT THE SUPERMARKET

Per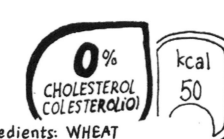

kcal
100
5%

0% CHOLESTEROL COLESTEROLiO)

kcal
50

GDA*

●Ingredients: WHEAT MOZZARELLA, EDAM), 7, flavouring), 7.2% mushroo olive oil, acids (calcium.ph emulsifier mono- and diacetyl raising agent sodium hydrogen oregano, garlic, herbs de Provence, dextrose.

' puree, water, rk, water, salt, dex palm fat, sugar, i calcium citrates), BARL tartaric acid esters of mono-and d carbonate, thickener guar gum,

At -18°C (✷✷✷ compartment or freezer) best before end: date If food has thawed, do not refreeze.

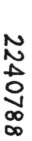

?

	Per 100 g	Per 1 Pizza (385g) (%*)	
Energy	888 kJ / 211 kcal	3419 kJ 1813 kcal (41%)	Fat of which saturates
Protein	8.3 g	31.9 g (64%)	Fibre
Carbohydrate of which sugars	28.1 g 2.5 g	108.1 g (40%) 9.6 g (11%)	Sodium (Na)

* Guideline Daily Amount (GDA) based on a 2000 kcal diet

Added

Vitamins and Minerals

e **380g**

?

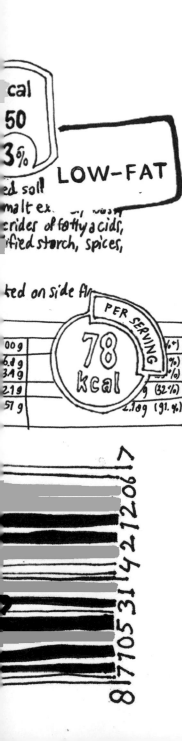

cal
50
3%

LOW-FAT

ed sol
malt ex
crides of fatty acids,
ified starch, spices,

ted on side fl

PER SERVING

78
kcal

00 g
6.d g
3.4 g
2.1 g   (32%)
.57 g   ..10 g (91.%)

8 7705 31 42 1206 17

Google

HOW to READ
the NUTRITION
FACTS LABEL

→ ABOUT 1,880,000 RESULTS
(0.29 SECONDS)

WHAT PACKAGING
would LOOK Like if...

03 ━━━━━━━━

WHAT PACKAGING WOULD LOOK LIKE IF...
only the description were left

*G*oogle "How to read the Nutrition Facts Label" and you'll be given over two million results. This could be considered evidence for the fact that labels on our food have not been created to make our lives easier.

There are regulations for the labelling of food products. However, if you want to get even more confused than the labels themselves might leave you, go ahead and read the Advertising Code of Health Products on packaging. The code was created by manufacturers, importers, retailers and advertising agencies (i.e. not consumers), and is fully incomprehensible to any sane mind. The code partly consists of lists with hundreds of quotes that are either classified as allowed or not allowed to be printed on packaging. For example, "Positive effect on heart and blood vessels" is not permitted, while "Beneficial effect on heart and blood vessels" is no problem at all. Incidentally, proof to support these statements is not required by the code.

Even if the Nutrition Facts Label was easier to understand, all the 'facts' it contains are based on one, commonly overlooked, piece of information: the 'serving size'. However, the serving size often has very little to do with what we actually consume. How often have you stopped eating crisps after one handful?

What packaging would look like if... Nutrition Facts Labels were made from a consumer's point of view?

29.1%

41.5%

29.4%

FAT   100%   100%   CARBOHYDRATE

100%

PROTEIN

WHAT PACKAGING WOULD LOOK LIKE IF...
nutritional values were translated into colour

0 kcal

100 kcal

WHAT PACKAGING WOULD LOOK LIKE IF...
the content were max. 100 kcal

WHAT PACKAGING WOULD LOOK LIKE IF...
only the nutrition facts were allowed

HOW DO WE *turn* FOOD *into* *a* PRODUCT?

04 ————

antioxidant (E300)

acid (E330)

Sugar

apples

APPLE SAUCE
Ingredients

*E*ach food product has its ingredients written on it, as this is mandatory. Processed foods show jaw-droppingly long lists of ingredients. Each one sounding worse than the next. National laws usually require processed food products to display a list of ingredients and specifically stipulate that certain additives must be listed. However, those additives are written in the tiniest font, almost unreadable.

Often these products taste good and look nicely manufactured, but we have no clue what we are really eating.
For instance, even though we eat it all the time, do we have any clue as to what emulsifier looks like? Or how about E340?

This chapter provides a visual for all the ingredients for a variety of products.

Roasted peanuts

Salt

dextrose

vegetable fat

vegetable oil

PEANUT BUTTER

Mustard Seed

Thickener
(xanthan gum)

Spices

Sugar

perservative (e202)

pigment
(carotene)

Salt

Citric acid

antioxidant (e385)

Natural vineger

vinegar

aroma

Rapeseed oil

free-range egg yolk

water

MAYONNAISE

Carbon dioxide

sugar

caffeine (powder)

phosphor

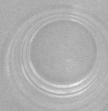

water

Sulphite ammonia caramel

Natural aroma

COLA

bay leaf

emulsifier (e472)

Stabiliser (e340)

tomato purée

sugar

onion powder

Spices

whipped cream

iodized salt

yeast extract

tomato

vegetable oil

Modified corn starch

(e451)

butter

concentrated
lemon juice

skimmed
milk powder

xanthan gum

vegetable fat

glucose syrup

wheat flour

flavour enhancer
(e621)

flavour

water

CREAM TOMATO SOUP

55

Salt

vegetarian rennet

starter

milk

BRIE

wheat flour

yeast

Sugar

baker's salt

rye flour

salt

bread crumbs

wheat gluten

dextrose

water

rye flour

BREAD

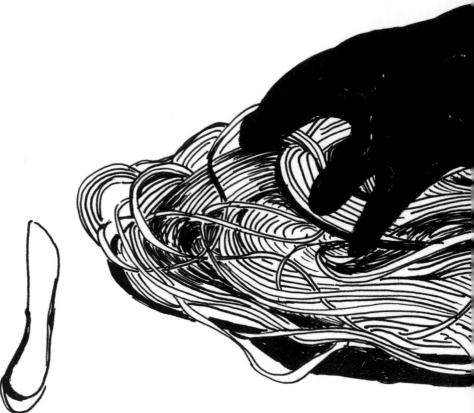

THE WORLD PRODUCE

to PROVIDE E

WITH MORE THAN

enough FOOD

ry PERSON

700 calories PER Day [3]

What is THE PRODUCTION size OF FOOD?

05 ———————

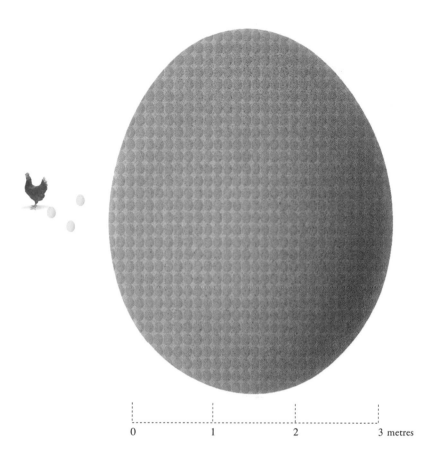

EGG PRODUCTION PER CHICKEN IN 5 YEARS
600-800 eggs [4]

---

*W*hen we see sugar beets growing in a field, we do not connect the dots and relate them to the sugar cubes we buy at the supermarket. When we walk around in the supermarket, putting food in our shopping cart, it's hard for us to realise how many hands, actions and operations our food has passed through to get there. There is a massive food industry behind all our food, which is neatly stocked on the shelves at eye level and with exactly the right (pre-cut) serving size.

The food industry is a complex, global collective of various businesses that supply much of the food energy consumed by the world's population. The average person in the western world eats 35 tons of food in a lifetime [5]. These figures are so massive, the amounts are almost unimaginable for us. Food production has become something we don't relate to at all anymore, even though it provides for one of our most basic needs.

Let's look at the production of our sustenance in a more comprehensible manner. How many eggs does 1 chicken lay in its life, or how many acres of grain do we need to produce 1 loaf of bread? You'll find the answers in this chapter.

width 4.5 metres

height 0.3 metres

length 6 metres

MILK PRODUCTION PER COW PER YEAR
8000 litres of milk [6]

0.95 metres

0.95 metres

M² GRAIN USED FOR 1 BREAD

0.8 m² grain [7]

SOFT DRINK PRODUCED PER MINUTE PER FACTORY
100 cans per minute [8]

1/3 of ALL FOOD is thrown out. [9]

HOW DISPOSABLE is OUR FOOD?

06 ——————

...8 days later

*O*n the one hand, it is fortunate that we no longer have to hunt for our food. On the other hand, we might appreciate our food more if we did, as it would be quite difficult to go out hunting with a shopping cart.
One third of our entire global food supply ends up thrown out. That adds up to about 100 kg per person each year! [10] Food has become an easily disposable product. Tomorrow you can simply replace that undesired food product with a new purchase... Because food is widely available and the shelves in the supermarket are always stocked with fresh products available at the lowest price, we seem to have forgotten the actual value of what we throw out on a regular basis.

We pull a face at the sight of a brown spot on our apple, but does that truly make it inedible? Next time you are shopping, take a look at the contents of your shopping cart and remember: a third of that will never be eaten. This chapter gives you a preview; what a waste!

71

...8 days later

...14 days later

...20 days later

...96 days later

...96 days later

...96 days later

Time you will have spent chewing

once you reach 75 [(11)]

DAYS	HOURS	MINUTES	SECONDS
308	05	23	08

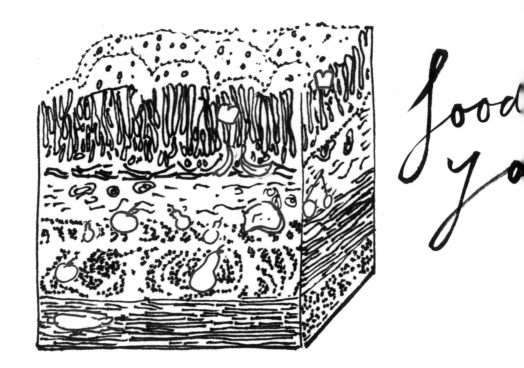

food
yo

Stays with
Longer than
you chew.

HOW (long) DO WE STORE OUR FOOD?

07 _____

~ esophagus ~

~ mouth ~

*Y*ou are what you eat? Well yes, you are, actually. You might even say literally so. Nutrition from food provides the building blocks for our bodies. Pinch your skin and remember that it has been created from the food you have eaten.

Food can also be considered fuel; it brings us from A to B. The energy and nutrients that our bodies need in order for us to live and work are obtained from food and beverages. Our bodies absorb liquid nutrition almost instantaneously, whereas solid food first needs to be broken down into particles small enough to travel through our bloodstream towards our cells. The breaking down of food is a mechanical and chemical process which is carried out by our digestive system in seven stages. [12]

Food stays with you longer than it takes for you to chew it.

For example, you can put a cookie in your mouth, maybe enjoy it for a few minutes and then forget all about it. But just because you can't see it anymore, doesn't mean it's really gone. It has just been moved and it continues to move through your body.

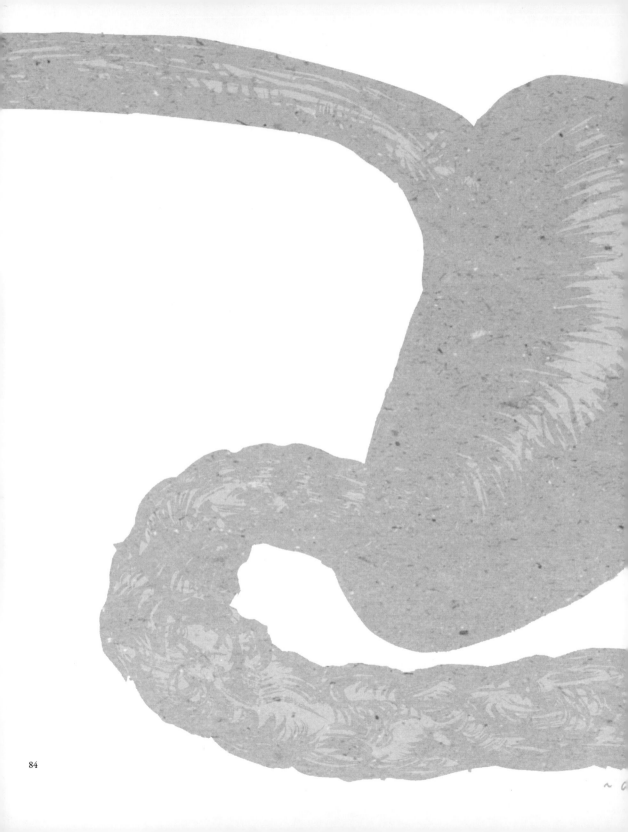

~ Stomach ~

~denum ~

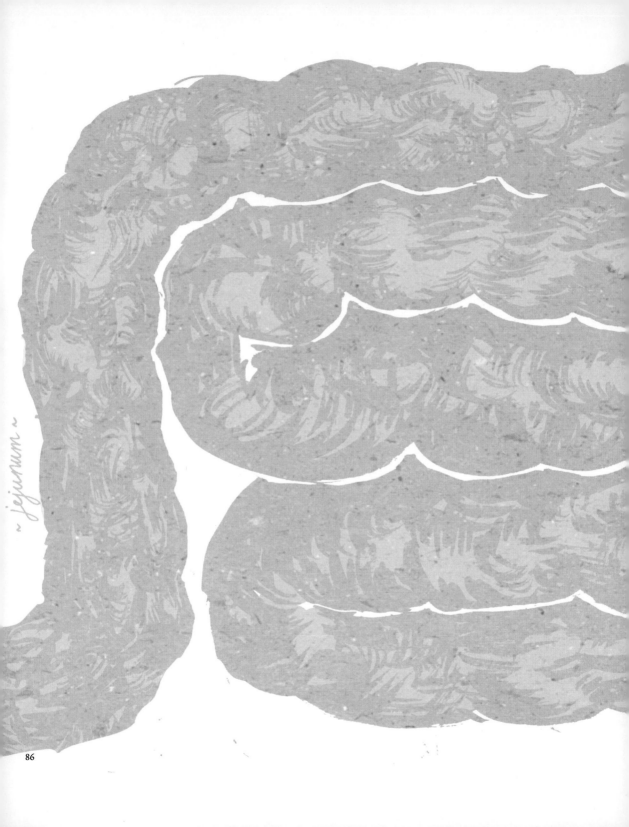

~ jejunum ~

~ jejunum ~

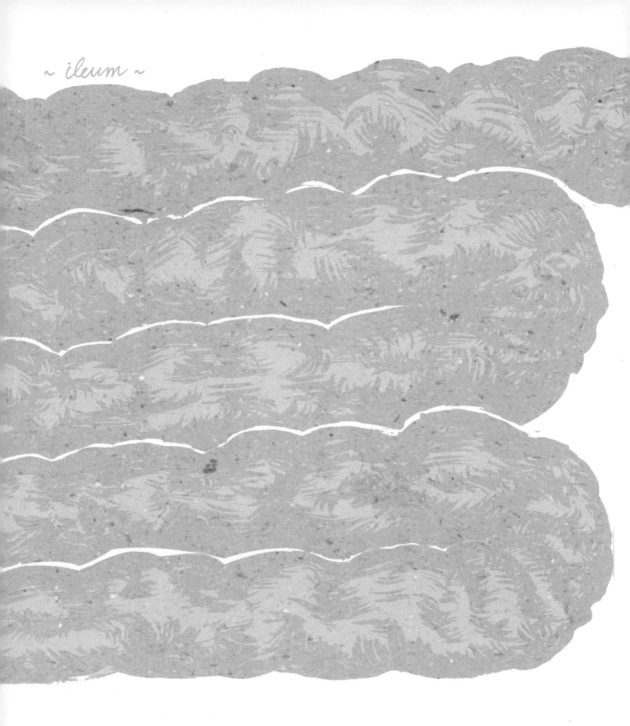

~ ileum ~

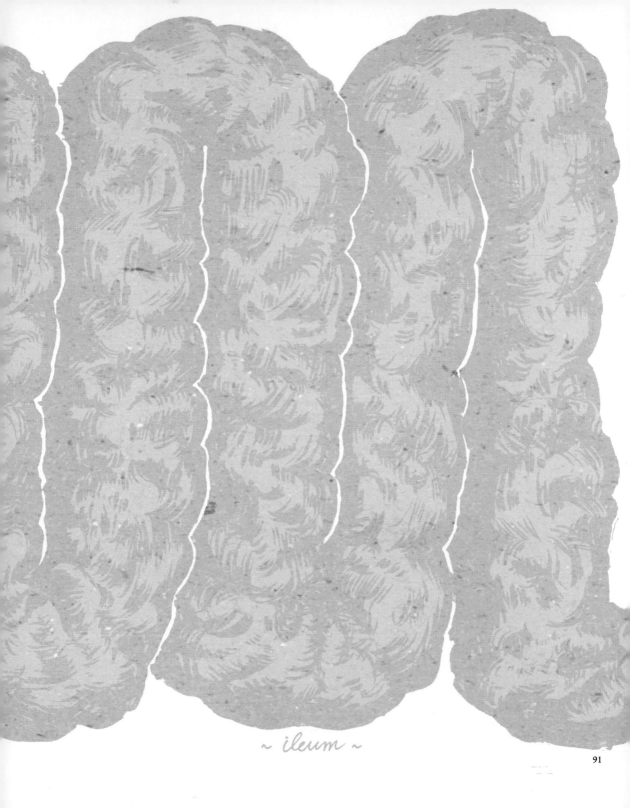

~ ileum ~

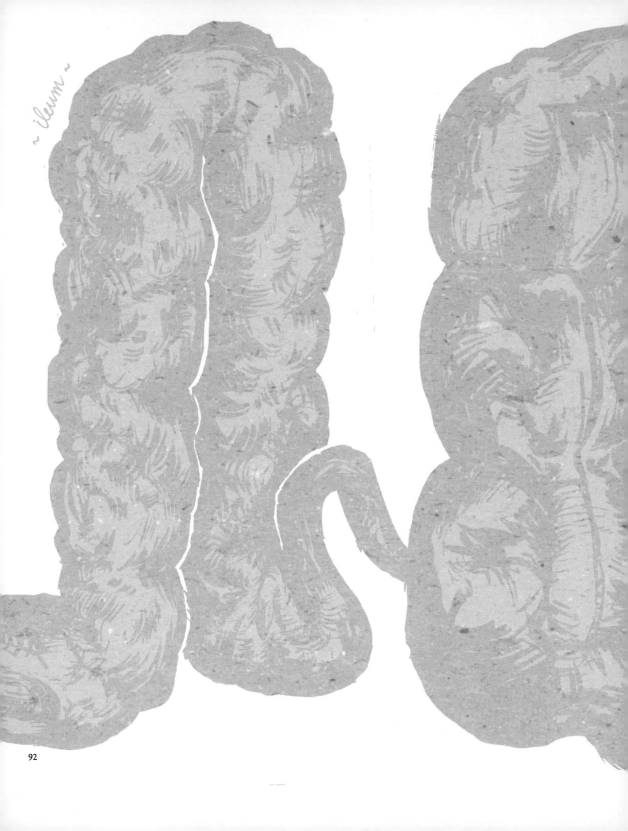

~ ileum ~

~ colon ~

~ appendix ~

94

~ colon ~

~ rectum ~

every year,
you gain
an average of
1 pound (13)

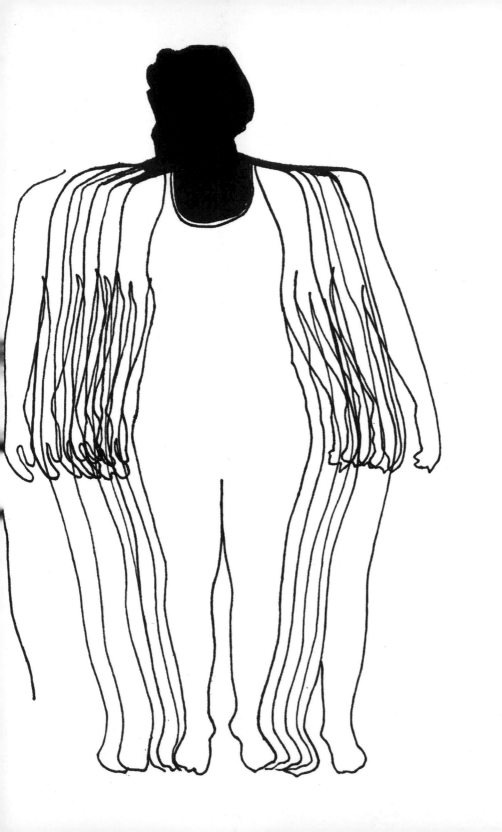

WHAT DOES a POUND a year LOOK LIKE?

08 ──────────

27 YEARS OLD
66 KILOS

+ 360 GRAMS A YEAR

52 YEARS OLD
75 KILOS

*O*ur society offers an abundance of food and eateries. At the same time, we are collectively trying to eat less; less fat, more diet products, following food gurus and methods to eat smaller portions or less frequently. After all, losing weight is good ("You look good; lost a few pounds?") and fat people are considered all kinds of wrong ("Look at that, she just keeps on eating...").

In today's western world, our appetite feels like our enemy. However, the need to eat fat is stored in our genes. This fat gene dates back to the Ice Age. At that time, the more fat reserves you had, the greater your chance of survival was. This stubborn fat gene seems to prevail over our current society's beauty ideal of having a slim figure.

On average, people in western countries gain 1 pound per year. [13] How disastrous! Slowly we grow and grow. Didn't these pants feel much looser last week...? If you look at photos from a few years ago, do you feel like you still looked thin back then? However, how happy were you with your body at that time? In short: is the concept of 'fat' truly on your hips or is it all just in your head?

Take a look at the following photo series; are those extra pounds really such a big deal?

99

25 YEARS OLD
78 KILOS

47 YEARS OLD
96 KILOS

+ 818 GRAMS A YEAR

35 YEARS OLD
62 KILOS

64 YEARS OLD
71 KILOS

+ 345 GRAMS A YEAR

22 YEARS OLD
100 KILOS

51 YEARS OLD
115 KILOS

+ 517 GRAMS A YEAR

IT'S HIS TIME
TO CALL - bar

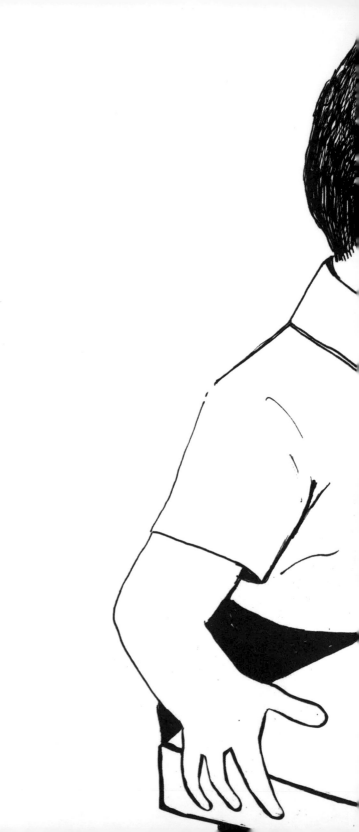

WHERE does
OUR APPETITE
Come FROM ?

09 ━━━━━━━━

1. Sandwiches and fruit   **8:45**

Breakfast is the most
important meal of the day

2. Coffee and biscuit   **10:45**

Coffee and a newspaper is the
best combination

3. Sandwiches and tea   **13:00**

Lunchtime, it's good to eat
on a schedule

4. Coffee and biscuit   **16:00**

I always drink coffee with a
biscuit this time of day

5. Fruit salad   **17:20**

Need to get my vitamins for
today

6. Kale with sausage   **18:15**

Dinner time, a hot meal
every day at 6

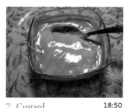

7. Custard   **18:50**

A sweet dessert, to get
a saturated feeling

8. Nuts and juice   **20:30**

A drink and a bite while
watching TV

9. Lemonade   **22:00**

I am a bit thirsty

ELDERLY LADY, AGE 78, WEIGHT 60 KG

*F*ood provides the building blocks for our bodies, acts as fuel and makes it possible for us to do the things we do. But there is another reason for our eating habits.

25% of the times at which we eat is dedicated to snacks [14].

What makes us eat a biscuit with our coffee or have a snack at the cinema? Why do we need to eat chocolate or crisps? Politeness, boredom, force of habit…? Simply because it is right there in front of you, it's tasty or you feel you deserve a treat. Our appetite is often more psychological than physical. Indeed, the psychological appetite seems a lot harder to satisfy…

Appetite is a feeling that has more to do with habituation or expectation than an actual physical NEED for sugars, vitamins and carbohydrates. If you have the habit of eating at 12 o'clock every day, your appetite will probably also emerge at that time.

Three people kept a food diary for one day, photographing everything they ate and drank and writing down why they did so. Take a closer look at the reasons behind their eating habits.

1. Energy drink   07:32

I'm extremely sleepy. So I got this at a gas station

2. Coffee   08:15

We always start the workday with coffee

3. Coffee   10:00

Coffee break

7. Sandwich   12:38

Not hungry, but eat to have energy later on in the day

8. Coffee   15:03

Coffee break

9. Chicken wrap   16:47

After a hard day's work, I reward myself by going through the McDrive

13. Lemonade   19:10

I'm thirsty

14. Pear   21:08

Unhealthy day today... I want to eat something healthy

15. Orange juice   22:10

I'm thirsty, so I'll drink something before I go to sleep

4. Instant soup   12:28

Lunch break, soup is provided at the
canteen

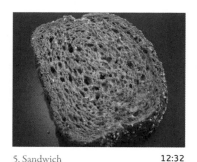

5. Sandwich   12:32

I need the energy, I haven't eaten
anything yet

6. Sandwich   12:34

Need some more energy

10. Burger   16:50

There is a good deal on burgers,
so I also take a burger

11. Spaghetti   18:19

Not so hungry anymore, but dinner is
served, so I eat

12. Ice cream   18:33

Do I want a dessert?
Yes, always! Tasty!

CONSTRUCTION WORKER, AGE 22, WEIGHT 65 KG

1. Sandwich   **08:00**

To be a good example for my kid,
I also eat a sandwich

2. Yoghurt drink   **08:01**

I drink this every
morning, tastes good

3. Rusk with chocolate   **08:05**

I like to finish my breakfast with
something sweet

7. Cheese and onion bread   **13:15**

Lunch with friends, we bought some
tasty bread

8. Sweet bun   **13:20**

I love sweet buns,
tastes really good

9. Sweet bun   **13:25**

Tastes great, I'll take another!

13. Banana   **16:00**

I feel a bit weak,
so I eat something

14. Grilled cheese sandwich   **18:50**

Dinner time, we don't feel
like cooking

15. Grilled cheese sandwich   **19:15**

Some more, one sandwich doesn't
make a complete dinner

4. Cracker with chocolate   **08:11**

I still crave something to eat

5. Diet Coke   **09:35**

Thirsty

6. Tea   **13:10**

We are having lunch with friends, starting with a cup of tea

10. Diet Coke   **14:05**

Don't want coffee or tea like the others, so I'll drink this

11. Candy   **15:00**

Feel like something sweet

12. Diet Coke   **15:50**

Thirsty

16. Crisps and 0% alcohol beer   **22:10**

To celebrate it's the weekend!

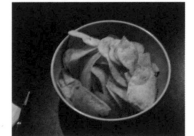

17. Crisps   **22:30**

A little bit more to finish the bag

PREGNANT WOMAN, AGE 31, WEIGHT 112 KG

A HAMBURGER is BIGGER than you THINK

550 kcal
BIG [15]

WHAT is THE TRUE SiZE of food?

Mars Bar (51 grams)

Nutritional values per 100 grams
fat: 16.6 grams
protein: 3.8 grams
carbohydrate: 70.1 grams

 1 KCAL CARBOHYDRATE   1 KCAL FAT   1 KCAL PROTEIN

---

*W*hat is more: A pound of sugar or a pound of potatoes? You might say that these are equal amounts; after all, a pound is a pound. But now take a look at the calories; those certainly do make a difference. 1 pound of sugar contains 2010 calories, whereas 1 pound of potatoes only has 420 calories. Our food is deceptive. Something might look like a small snack, but could contain the same number of calories as a full dinner.

Wouldn't it be convenient to have a visual nutrition table that could show you at a glance how much you really eat? It would certainly leave more of an impression than the usual list of nutritional values.

4 kcal = 1 gram carbohydrate
9 kcal = 1 gram fat
4 kcal = 1 gram protein [16]

121

Cola (330 ml)

Nutritional values per 100 ml
fat: 0 ml
protein: 0 ml
carbohydrate: 10.6 ml

Sweet pepper crisps (20 grams)

Nutritional values per 100 grams
fat: 36 grams
protein: 6.5 grams
carbohydrate: 52 grams

 1 KCAL CARBOHYDRATE   1 KCAL FAT   1 KCAL PROTEIN

Hamburger (92 grams)

Nutritional values per 100 grams
fat: 9 grams
protein: 13 grams
carbohydrate: 30 grams

Wholemeal bread (35 grams)

Nutritional values per 100 grams
fat: 1.5 grams
protein: 8.5 grams
carbohydrate: 44 grams

Rusk (11 grams)

Nutritional values per 100 grams
fat: 4.5 grams
protein: 14 grams
carbohydrate: 77 grams

Aniseed (35 grams)

Nutritional values per 100 grams
fat: 0 grams
eiwit: 2 grams
carbohydrate: 90 grams

 1 KCAL CARBOHYDRATE  1 KCAL FAT  1 KCAL PROTEIN

Pink cake (55 grams)

Nutritional values per 100 grams
fat: 21 grams
protein: 4 grams
carbohydrate: 60 grams

Pear (158 grams)

Nutritional values per 100 grams
fat: 0 grams
protein: 2.5 grams
carbohydrate: 17.5 grams

 1 KCAL CARBOHYDRATE    1 KCAL FAT    1 KCAL PROTEIN

Potato (119 grams)

Nutritional values per 100 grams
fat: 0 grams
protein: 2 grams
carbohydrate: 17.6 grams

French fries (189 grams)

Nutritional values per 100 grams
fat: 7.7 grams
protein: 10 grams
carbohydrate: 43 grams

 1 KCAL CARBOHYDRATE 1 KCAL FAT 1 KCAL PROTEIN

Pork fillet (142 grams)

Nutritional values per 100 grams
fat: 5.9 grams
protein: 22.7 grams
carbohydrate: 0 grams

Steak (151 grams)

Nutritional values per 100 grams
fat: 1.5 grams
protein: 25 grams
carbohydrate: 0 grams

Egg (61 grams)

Nutritional values per 100 grams
fat: 11.2 grams
protein: 12.9 grams
carbohydrate: 0.7 grams

Chicken leg (75 grams)

Nutritional values per 100 grams
fat: 11.3 grams
protein: 25.5 grams
carbohydrate: 0 grams

 1 KCAL CARBOHYDRATE   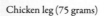 1 KCAL FAT   1 KCAL PROTEIN

When we consider
a certain food item
TO BE GOOD FOR US
it may lead
to OVEREATING
which is BAD for US

COMPARING apples TO MARS bars

11 —————

Apple

Mars bar

EXPIRATION DATE (DAYS) [17]

---

*H*ealthy versus unhealthy. We've learned this growing up: First eat your broccoli, then you can have a dessert. The supermarket is also organised in this manner: The fruit and vegetable section versus the candy aisle. You prefer to make conscious choices, which means you know exactly which aisles to avoid. However, it seems as though it has already been determined for you what you should consider healthy or unhealthy choices.

But what does 'healthy' mean anyway?
When you compare books on nutrition, you will notice that they do not all say the same thing.

What one book promotes as being 'healthy' can be described as very 'unhealthy' in another. For example, is bread healthy or not? Are dairy products good or bad for you?

Our food is not simply healthy or unhealthy. It consists of many characteristics that are considered valuable to a greater or lesser degree, depending on the context in which they are discussed. In an attempt to put the health debate into perspective, this chapter provides you with several examples of views on food, offering you input for drawing your own conclusions.

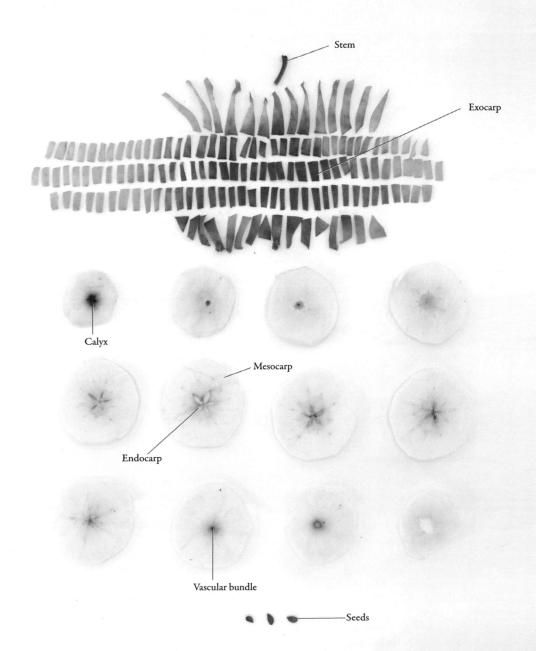

Chocolate

Nougat

Caramel

ANATOMY

Apple (143 grams)

Mars bar (55 grams)

1 BATTERY IS 4 KCAL

Appel
apple
Mela
Manzana
pomme
apfel
яблоко
تفاح
苹果
apæ̃a
appel
Mollë
Mazana
ᏘᎤᏗ
alma
алма
sagar
póm
Maila
Maçä
aval
яблъка
яблык
puma
pumu
poba
brondá
poma
lax
Rfw
jabuka

jabiko
jabko
æble
تفاح
ponma
pomo
õun
apli
süvepli
yapolo
omena
apel
miluz
miluç
mēi
ვაშლი
ύήλο
iipili
milo
masã
guavirana'a
یاسیب
ãfŭl
'ãhia
ãpala
תפוח
सेब
kxiverpaum
epli
üll
 סה
ipome

তটি
선
sen
ຫັມ
pòm
pomum
âbols
obuolys
pòmm
jaborka
pòma
epal
šŭffŭha
ooyl
āpoгo
सफरचंद
Mаpь
алин
pàm
méla
eple
μήλον
تفاح
apula
jablko
maçã
mila
उँ
pòm
mèila
Mär

mail
ẽppel
apu
सेब
meba
ubhal
jaбyka
apole
ápwro
li-hhábhula
jabolko
tufaox
tufaha
äpple
öpfel
Mansánas
ceб
kaʋɛʋa
'qele
頻果
pomo
ānma
яблуко
опта
mel'
quả táo
pod
ofal
iapule
אפל
ápú

èso
òзo
àyembò
meia
iapula
ihabhula

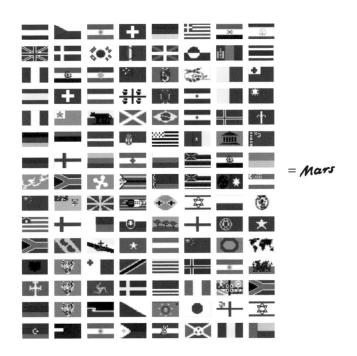 = *Mars*

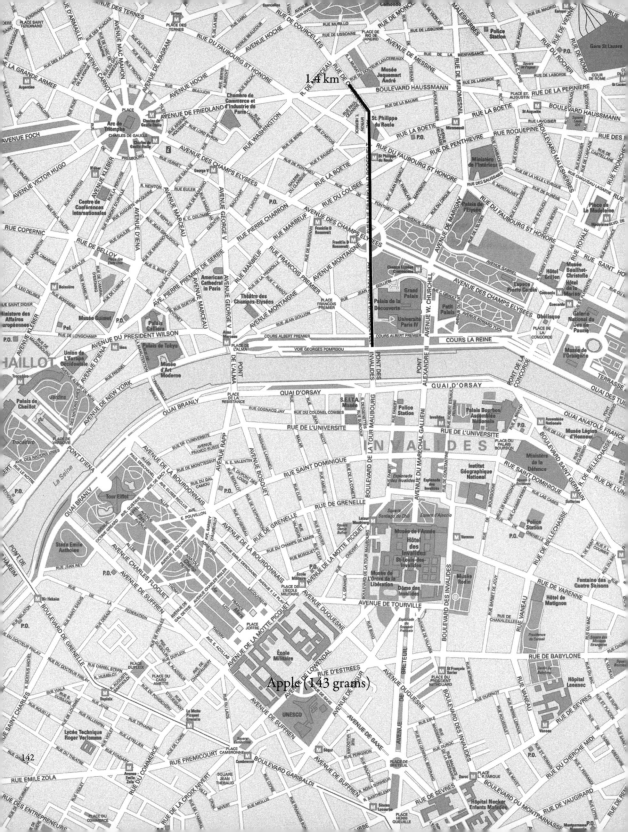

1.4 km

Apple (143 grams)

142

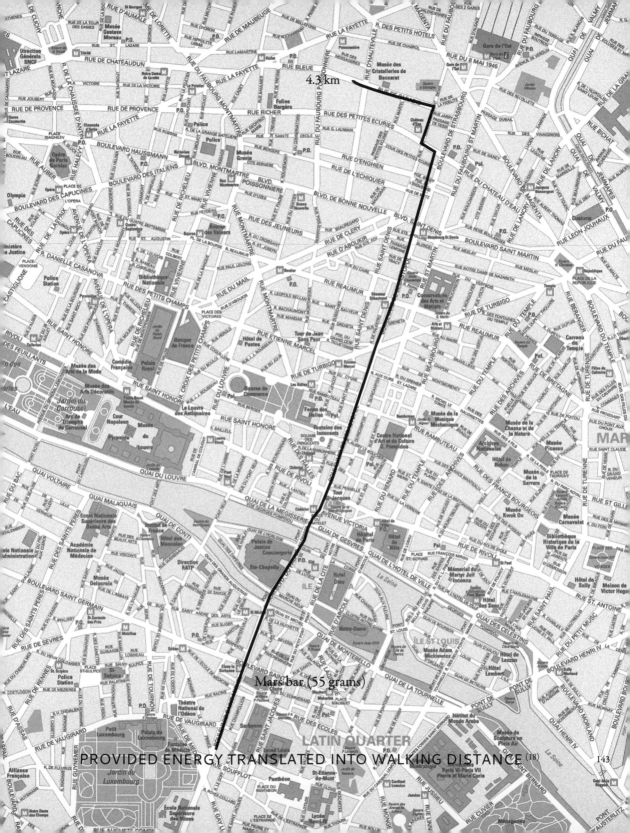

4.3 km

Mars bar (55 grams)

PROVIDED ENERGY TRANSLATED INTO WALKING DISTANCE [18]

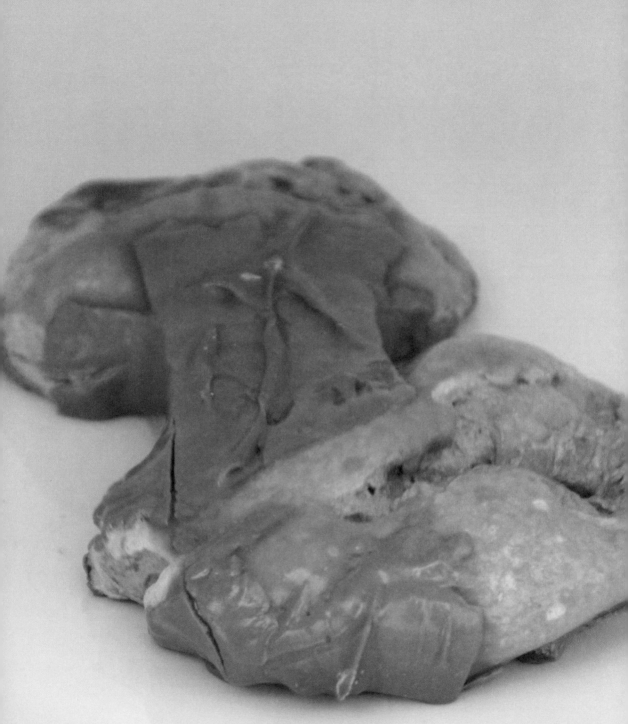

MICROWAVE – 800 WATT

bite 1

bite 2

bite 3

bite 4

bite 5

bite 6

bite 7

bite 8

bite 9

bite 10

bite 11

bite 12

fin 4.20 min.

bite 1

bite 2

bite 3

fin 1.52 min.

CONSUMING TIME

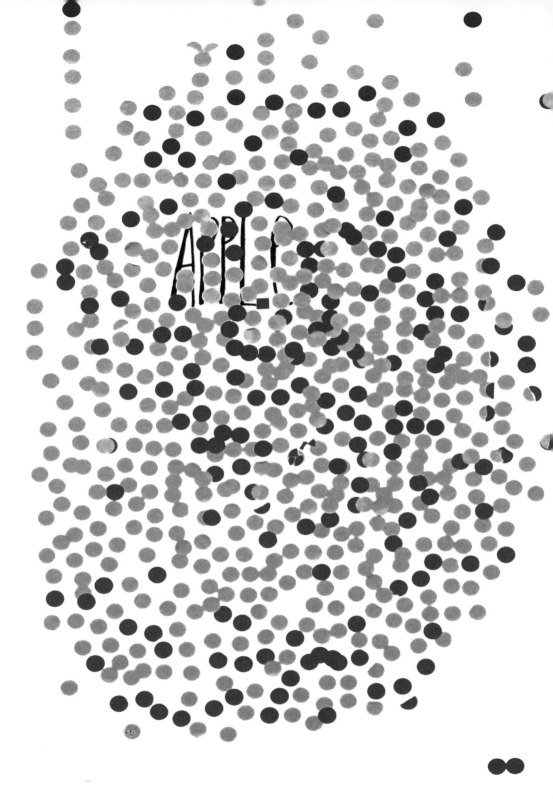

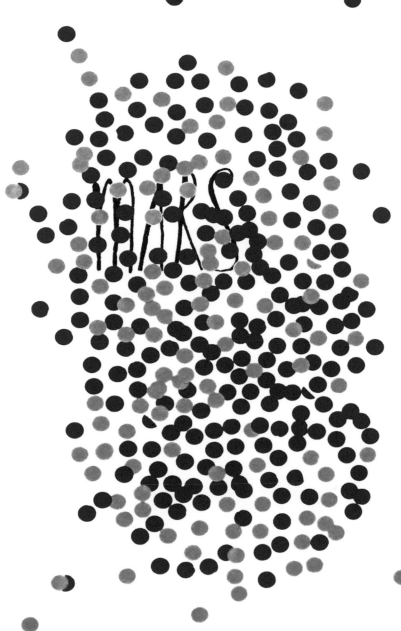

People were asked:
Which do you prefer, an apple or a Mars bar?
You want a red or a green sticker to vote?

PREFERENCE SURVEY

Minerals

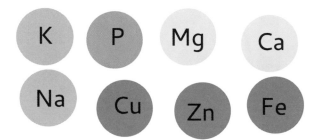

Vitamins

Apple

Minerals

Vitamins

Mars bar

VITAMINS AND MINERALS (19)

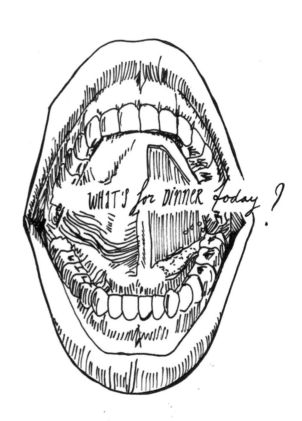

- [1] (page 29)
We spend 60 hours a year in a supermarket.
Source: http://www.cbl.nl/de-supermarktbranche/feiten-
en-cijfers/supermarktbezoeken/

- [2] (page 31)
Analysis shows that the top four western food companies
control a substantial majority of the global sales of food
products, often offering multiple brands for each type of
grocery.
Source: http://documents.foodandwaterwatch.org/doc/
grocery_goliaths.pdf

Ingredients products (page 51-57)
Apple sauce: Spar brand
Peanut butter: Vita D'or Lidl
Mayonnaise: Albert Heijn
Cola: Freeway Aldi
Tomato cream soup: Albert Heijn
Brie: Euroshopper, Albert Heijn
Bread: white tiger bread Lidl

- [3] (page 59)
The world can produce enough food to provide every
person with more than 2 700 calories per day.
Source: http://www.fao.org/docrep/x0262e/x0262e05.
htm

- [4] (page 61)
Egg production per chicken in 5 years (600-800 eggs).
Source: http://wiki.answers.com/Q/How_many_eggs_
do_hens_lay_on_average

- [5] (page 61)
The average person in the western world eats 35 tons of
food in a lifetime.
Source: http://www.omg-facts.com/Animals/The-average-
person-eats-35-tons-of-food/46325

- [6] (page 63)
Milk production per cow per year (8000 litres).
Source: http://homepage.tinet.ie/~agatha/dairy_herd.htm

- [7] (page 65)
0.8 M² Grain used for 1 bread. About 9000 kilos of wheat per acre is harvested from a field. Sometimes even more. 100 kilos of grain is enough for about 120 loaves.
Source: http://www.akkerbouw.info/pdf/graandocent.pdf

- [8] (page 67)
Soft drink produced per minute per factory (Wakefield factory (UK)) (100 cans).
Source: http://www.cokecce.co.uk/about-us/sites-and-offices/wakefield.aspx

- [9] (page 69)
1/3 of all food is thrown out.
Source: http://www.fao.org/news/story/en/item/196220/icode/

- [10] (page 71)
One third of our entire global food supply ends up thrown out. That adds up to about 100 kg per person each year.
Source: http://en.wikipedia.org/wiki/Food_waste

- [11] (page 79)
Time you will have spent chewing, once you reach 75: 308 days.
Counted with an average of 20 minutes a day.

- [12] (page 83)
The breaking down of food is a mechanical and chemical process which is carried out by our digestive system in seven stages.
Source: http://en.wikipedia.org/wiki/Digestion

- [13] (page 96)
Every year you gain an average of 1 pound.
Source: Arbo Magazine 24 - 04-04-2008 - Koen Zonneveld

- [14] (page 113)
25% of the times at which we eat is dedicated to snacks.
Source: http://www.livescience.com/14769-snacking-calories-increase.html

- [15] (page 119)
Burger contains 550 kcal.
Source: http://nutrition.mcdonalds.com/getnutrition/nutritionfacts.pdf

- [16] (page 121)
1 gram carbohydrate = 4 kcal
1 gram fat = 9 kcal
1 gram protein = 4 kcal
Source: http://en.wikipedia.org/wiki/Food_energy

Nutrition facts (page 121-131)
Source: Package label information + http://www.voedingswaardetabel.nl/

- [17] (page 135)
Expiration date (days).
Source: label packaging

- [18] (page 143)
Provided energy translated into walking distance.
5 kcal per minute at a speed of 5.6 km / h

- [19] (page 151)
Vitamins and minerals apple and Mars bar.
Source: http://www.voedingswaardetabel.nl/

index

The True Size of Food

CONCEPT
PHOTOGRAPHY
ILLUSTRATION
GRAPHIC DESIGN
} Marijke Timmerman

TEXT {
Charlotte Poorskamp,
Loes Timmerman &
Marijke Timmerman

TRANSLATION and CORRECTIONS   Sorina Bouwhuis

Special THANKS:

ROB VERHOFSTAD
KARIN TIMMERMAN
WIM KUPER
MARLÉNE NIJHUIS
NICOLE DIJBRANDIJ
SASKIA SCHREVEN
KASIA ZAREBA
MATHILDE ALDERS
HANNAH VISCHER
JOZEE BROUWER
and everyone else who
contributed their time
and expertise

portraits a pound per year:
Arnoud Ruesink, Ellen Dijkstra
Fini verhofstad, henk Teela
Pia van de Sande, Myriam Wensing

food diaries: Rob verhofstad,
Renée Timmerman, jannie oonk
Eldert van het Hof, jet Timmerman,
Ell Koumans van Bellecum

CREDITS